""This book portrays a nostalgic look at wild life and country scenes gathered from the Joubert's travels around Alberta and British Columbia. It evokes images of a simpler, quite life that a lot of us would love to experience. Christine and her family left BC in 1978 for Calgary and quickly made a life for themselves in the building and food industry, wood working, painting, graphic arts and photography. ALSO QUICK TO DEVELOP THEIR LOVE OF THE OUT DOORS Collaborating with her talented daughters Cindy and Nicole. Christine has skillfully mixed her unique style of graphics with stunning photographs. Home cooked recipes that she has gathered from her research into country cooking plus several she has invented herself, are presented on a background of remarkable photography contributed by the entire Joubert clan. Wholesome, quick meals that mostly can be put together in 30 to 40 minutes, along with traditional breads and desserts, are fondly presented for the busy families of today. Christine and her husband Garry look forward to continuing their exploration of the spectacular scenery around Calgary as she plans her future books."

Email Christine at prairiestone@ shaw.ca

Garry's Photo/08

Baking

Plum Coffee Cake

Cream together 3/4 cup sugar, 1/2 cup margarine, 1 egg and 1 tsp. vanilla. Sift together 1 1/4 cup flour, 2 tsp. baking powder, 1/2 tsp. salt. Alternate with 1/2 cup milk with dry ingredients to egg mixture. Pour into a square pan. Top with rows of plum slices. Combine 1/2 cup firmly packed brown sugar, 3 tb. flour, 1/2 tsp. cinnamon 1/4 cup chopped walnuts until crumbly, sprinkle on top of plums. Bake at 375 for 35 to 40 minutes or until done with a toothpick test. Cool to warm before cutting into squares.

My photos / 08

4

Sweet Potato Biscuits

In a bowl mix 1 1/4 cup self rising flour, 2 tb. sugar, 3/4 cup cooked and mashed sweet potato along with 1 stick butter, mix with hands until mixture resembles corn meal. Add 1/4 cup milk, mix just enough to incorporate, cut into biscuits. Bake in a 350 oven for 25 to 30 minuties. Brush with a butter honey mixture.

Honey mixture...... 1/3 cup liquid honey, mix with 1/4 cup butter. mix well.

Garrys photo/08

Low Cal Pumpkin Torte

Sift together 2 1/2 cups cake flour, 3 tsp. baking powder, 2 tsp. pumpkin spice, 1/2 tsp. cinnamon, 1/2 tsp. butter flavored salt set aside. Combine 6 egg yolks, 2/3 cup light margarine, 1 can pumpkin, 3/4 cup firm packed brown sugar, 2/3 cup equal sugar, beat until smooth, gradually add dry ingredients to wet mixture. Beat 6 egg whites and 1/2 tsp. cream tarter until stiff, fold in pumpkin mixture. Pour into a greased tube pan. Bake at 350 for 60 minutes. Cool on rack. 160 cal. 1 serving.

6

My photo

Easy Breezy White Bread

In a small bowl stir to dissolve 2 tb. yeast in 1 cup of warm water along with 1 tsp. sugar. Let stand for 10 minutes. Mix yeast mixture into 4 cups warm water, 1/2 cup sugar, 1 tb. salt and 1/2 cup margarine until all has dissolved. Add 9 cups flour 1 cup at a time, mixing with a hand mixer until dough climbs beaters. Use a wooden spoon to beat until all flour has been used up. Turn onto a floured board and knead until dough has become smooth. Place in a greased large bowl, knead again. Place in a warm place, until double size. Punch down. Shape into loafs, rise again. Bake in a preheated 400 oven for 20 to 35 minutes, or until golden brown.

My Photos/08

7

Texas Chocolate Cake

Combine 1 3/4 cup flour, 2 cups sugar, 1/2 tsp. salt, 1 tsp. baking soda and 1/2 cup sour cream. In a sauce pan bring 2 tb butter, 1 cup water, and 4 tb. cocoa to a boil. Add to flour mixture, mix well. Pour into a greased 9x13x2 oblong floured baking pan. Bake at 350 for 20 to 30 minutes or until done with a toothpick test.

Icing

1 lb. powdered sugar, 1 cup chopped walnuts. In a sauce pan bring 1 tb. butter, 6 tb. milk, 4 tb cocoa to a boil. Add at once to sugar mixture and mix thoroughly. Ice cake while hot.

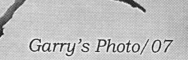

8 Garry's Photo/07

Treasure Toffee Cake

Combine 1/4 cup sugar, 1 tsp. cinnamon, set aside. Mix 2 cups flour, 1 cup sugar, 1 1/2 tsp. baking powder, 1 tsp. baking soda, 1/4 tsp. salt in a large bowl. Mix in a bowl 1 cup sour cream, 1 tsp. vanilla. 1/2 cup soft butter and 2 eggs. Blend at low speed into flour, adding a little at a time. Spoon 1/2 of batter into a greased and floured bundt pan. Sprinkle with 2 tb. cinnamon mixture. Spoon remaining batter into pan. Top with remaining cinnamon mixture with 1/4 cup chopped nuts, 3 bars of coarsely chopped chocolate toffee bars, 1/4 cup powdered sugar mixed on top. Pour 1/4 cup melted butter over top. Bake in a 325 oven for 45 to 50 minutes. cool 15 minutes before removing from pan. Dust with powdered sugar.

My photo

My morning visitor/08

Blueberry Corn Muffins

Blend 1 8 ounce pack. corn muffin mix, 1 tb. brown sugar, 1 egg and 1/3 cup milk. Batter should be slightly lumpy. Stir in 1/2 cup blueberries.

Fill a greased muffin tin half full. Bake in a preheated oven at 400 for 15 to 20 min. until golden brown. Makes 10 to 12 muffins.

10

Garry's photo/08

Coffee Bread Cake

I bag frozen bread balls placed in around a buttered bundt pan, sprinkle 1 box of jello butter scotch pudding mix, 1/2 cup brown sugar evenly on top. Pour 1/2 cup melted butter evenly over all surfaces. Sprinkle again with 1 cup chopped mixed nuts. Cover with a damp cloth and let stand to rise over night. Should have filled the pan. Bake in a preheated oven at 350 for 30 minutes.

11

My Photo/08

Quince Bars

Cream 3/4 cup room temperature butter, 1 cup sugar, 1 egg, and 1 1/2 tsp. vanilla. Mix together 1/2 tsp. salt, 1 cup flour and 1 1/2 cup shredded coconut, stir well to blend. Reserve 3/4 cup for topping. Spread remaining mixture in a greased 9x10 inch pan. Spread apricot jam over mixture. Sprinkle 1 cup coarsely chopped walnuts over jam. Crumble reserved dough over top. Bake in a preheated 350 oven for 30 minutes. Cool. Cut into 24 bars.

Cindy's flower

My Photo/ Graphics
Nics Butterfly 08

12

Applesauce and Raisin Bread

Stir together 2 cups flour, 1 tb. baking powder, 1 tsp. salt, 1 tsp. cinnamon and 1/2 tsp. cloves. Combine 1 cup unsweetened applesauce, 2 beaten eggs, 1/4 cup brown sugar packed, 1/4 cup vegetable oil, stir in 1 cup raisins and 1/2 cup finely chopped nuts. Add to the flour mixture, stir just until moistened. Pour into a greased loaf pan. Bake in a 350 oven for 50 to 55 minutes or until done, cool in pan for 15 minutes before removing. Makes 1 loaf.

13

My Photo/06

Blueberry Loaf

Cream 1/4 lb. soften margarine and 3/4 cup sugar until blended, beat in 1 egg. Stir in 1/2 cup milk, 1 tsp. vanilla. In another bowl mix 2 cups flour, 2 tsp. baking powder, 1/2 tsp. salt. Stir to mix evenly. Stir in to egg and margarine mixture just to incorporate, fold in 1 small basket of blue berries. Pour into a well greased loaf pan and bake in a 350 oven for 45 to 60 minutes, use a toothpick tester for doneness.

My photo/08

Garry's photo/06

Cherry Coconut Slices

Combine 1 cup flour, 1/2 cup butter, 2 tb. icing sugar to make a shortbread base. Pat into a buttered 9x9 pan. Bake at 350 for 10 minutes. Combine 1 1/2 cups brown sugar, 2 well beaten eggs, 1/2 cup chopped walnuts, 8 oz. halved maraschino cherries, 1/2 cup coconut, 1/2 cup baking powder and 1/2 tsp. almond extract. Pour over cooled base. Bake for 25 to 30 minutes or until done. Cool then cover with a thin butter icing or cherry icing using cherry syrup with icing sugar. Cut into squares.

Garry's Photo/ 07

pavlova

Beat 4 eggs whites, 1/4 tsp. salt, and 1/2 tsp. cream of tarter until stiff. Add 1 1/4 cups white sugar slowly, tb. spoon full at a time, mixture should be satiny. Add 1 tsp vanilla and 1 tsp lemon juice. Spread on tin foil in a heart shape, or any shape. Place in a preheated oven at 375, close door and turn off heat, leave over night. Do not peek. When ready to serve place on a serving plate. Cover with whipped cream and garnish with fresh fruit of strawberries, blueberries, peaches, melons, kiwis or mandarin orange.

16

Garry's photo

Irish Soda Bread

Sift 2 cups flour, 1 tb. sugar, 1 1/2 tsp. baking powder, 1 tsp. baking soda and 1/2 tsp. salt into a large bowl. Cut in 1/4 cup margarine until resembles course meal.   Stir in 3/4 cup raisins, add 1 cup butter milk, blend just to moisten dry ingredients. Turn onto a floured board. Knead for 4 to 5 minutes until smooth. Place dough ball onto a greased baking sheet. Flatten to 1 1/2 inch thick, brush with a egg water mixture. Cut with a sharp knife individual sections. Bake in a 375 oven for 30 to 40 minutes. Transfer to a wire rack.

My Photos/08

17

Cream Puffs

Combine 1 cup water with 1/2 cup oil in a pan and bring to a boil. In a bowl beat lightly 4 eggs. Add 1 cup flour, 1 tsp. baking powder to oil mixture. Mix with a wooden spoon to form a ball, remove from heat. Add beaten eggs and mix well until smooth and soften. Drop from a tsp. onto a floured baking sheet, 12 per sheet. Bake in a 400 oven, checking frequently for a light brown. Custard Filling..........................
In a blender mix 1/2 cup sugar, 2 cups milk, 5 tsp flour, 2 egg yolks and a pinch salt and 1 tsp. vanilla until smooth. Pour into a double boiler. Cook slowly to thicken. Pipe with a large tip into puffs.

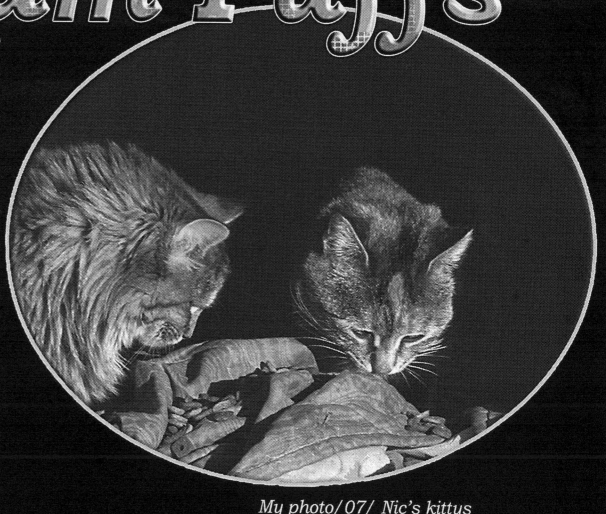

My photo/07/ Nic's kittys

18

Jam Squares

Place 1/2 cup butter in a sauce pan and melt. Remove from heat, add 1/2 cup sugar with 1 egg. Whisk well, Mix in 1 1/2 cup flour and 1 tsp. baking powder. Spread evenly in a square greased pan.

Garry's photo/07

Spread 1/2 cup of any flavour jam evenly over top. In a bowl mix 1 egg, 1/4 cup sugar and 1 cup coconut, mix well. Sprinkle and spread over jam. Bake in a preheated oven for 30 minutes. Cool in pan before cutting.

Lazy Daisy Cake

Scald 1/2 cup milk with 1 tb. butter, cool slightly. In another mixing bowl, beat 2 eggs for 2 to 3 minutes, add 1 cup sugar, beating constantly. Add 1 tsp. vanilla. Mix in 1 cup flour, 1 tsp. baking powder and 1/4 tsp. salt. Add milk mixture to flour mixture.
Pour into a greased floured cake pan. Bake in a 350 oven for 30 minutes or until done from a toothpick test.

Topping.........   In a small sauce pan mix 3 tb. butter, 2/3 cup brown sugar and 2 tb. milk until it comes to a boil. Pour over cake. Sprinkle with 1/2 cup shredded coconut. Place under a broiler until it bubbles. Remove and cool 5 to 10 minutes and serve.

20

My photos/ 06

Koeksisters

Sift together 2 cups flour, 3 tsp. baking powder, 1/2 tsp. salt. Rub with hands 2 tb. soft butter, 1 tb. margarine mixing into flour mixture along with a mixture of 1/2 cup water and 1 egg whisk together to make a soft dough. Roll out dough to 1/4 inch thick, cut into 2x2 squares.

Make a small cut in the centre of each square and twist one end of square through the cut to make a twist shape. Fry in 2 inches of hot oil until golden brown, remove and dip into cold syrup, cover on all sides, drain on a wire rack. Syrup...
1 cup water, 2 cups sugar a few broken pieces of cinnamon stick. Stir until sugar has dissolved in the boiling sugar water mixture.

My photos/graphic/07

Tangy Fruit Cake

Nic's butterfly

Cream 1/2 cup butter and 3/4 cup sugar until fluffy. Beat in 2 eggs 1 at a time, beat well after each egg. Add 1 tb. lemon rind and 1 tsp. lemon extract. Sift together 1 2/3 cup cake flour, 1 1/2 tsp. baking powder and 1/4 tsp. salt. Add dry ingredients alternately with 2/3 cup milk, beat with a mixer on medium speed. Began and end with dry ingredients.

Pour batter into a greased and floured mold ring pan. Bake in a preheated 325 oven for 30 to 40 minutes. Cool on rack for 10 to 15 minutes before loosening edges. Fill center with fresh berries and top with whipped topping.

22

Cindy's photo/ my graphics

Breakfast

Gopher in The Hole

Mix in a bowl 1 cup flour, 1 tsp. baking powder, 1 egg, salt and pepper. Mix all together to the consistency of a thick cream. Pour over 6 cooked sausages in a greased pie dish.   Bake in a 350 oven for 20 minutes or until golden brown. Serve with Maple syrup or brown sugar sprinkled on top.

cindy's gopher

MY photo/08

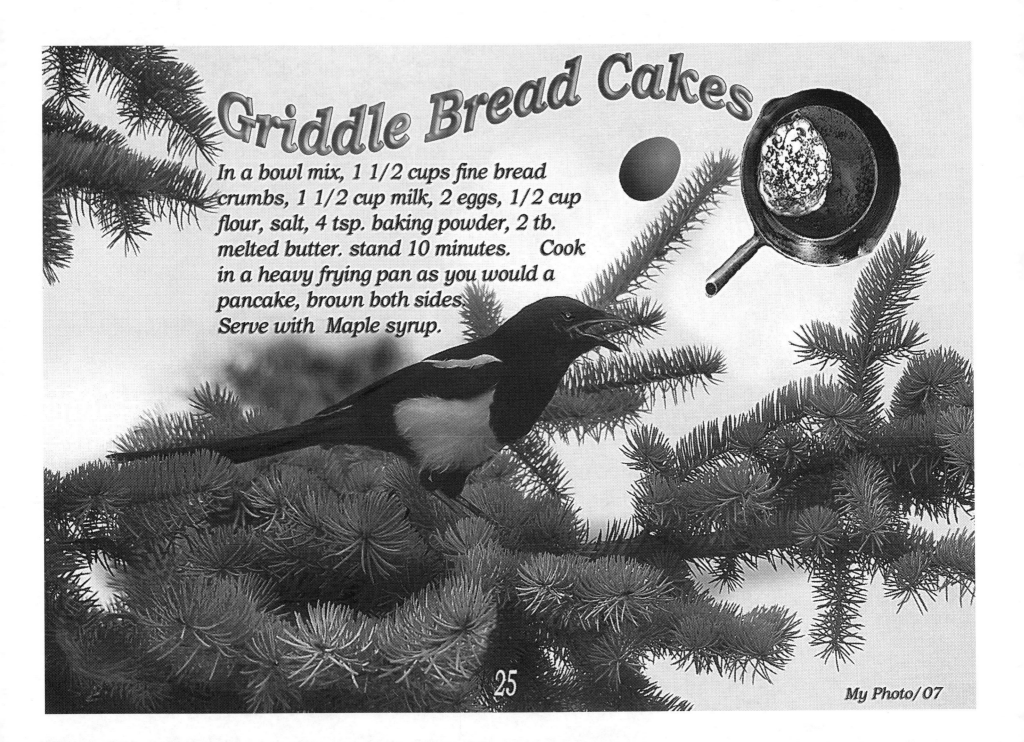

Griddle Bread Cakes

In a bowl mix, 1 1/2 cups fine bread crumbs, 1 1/2 cup milk, 2 eggs, 1/2 cup flour, salt, 4 tsp. baking powder, 2 tb. melted butter. stand 10 minutes.   Cook in a heavy frying pan as you would a pancake, brown both sides. Serve with Maple syrup.

25

My Photo/07

Bread Omelet

Soak 3/4 cup bread crumbs in 1/2 cup milk. Let stand for 5 minutes. In a bowl beat 3 egg yolks lightly. In another beat 3 egg whites until stiff. Drain excess milk from crumbs, beat into egg yolks, add 1/2 tsp. salt, fold in egg whites. Melt 1 tb. butter in a frying pan, pour in the mixture and cook on high heat for 1 minute. Reduce heat, cover and let cook on low for 15 to 20 minutes, fold on to a serving plater.

corn Fritters

Mix 1 can cream of corn, 3 tb. flour, 2 tb. baking powder, 1 beaten egg, 1/2 tsp. salt and pepper. Mix to incorporate. Drop mixture into a greased medium hot skillet with a round spoon. When bubbles start to form, flip to brown the other side. Serve with sour cream or syrup.

Nic's Photo

Eggs Orientale

In a sauce Pan bring 3 cups water and 1 tb. white vinegar to a boil. Break 4 eggs into a dish gently then into the boiling water gently, pouch for 3 1/2 minutes. Remove with a slotted spoon and set aside in a warm dish. In a sauce pan, melt 1 tb. butter on a high heat until it foams, reduce heat and saute 4 slices tomato slices into butter, on each side. Arrange into a buttered baking dish. Place each egg on a tomato slice and season well. Cover with Hollandaise sauce.

Bake in oven 4" away from broiling element for 3 minutes...............................
Sauce...Place 2 egg yolks in a double boiler. Whisk in 2 tb. water. With almost boiling water, whisk until thickened. Add 3/4 cup melted butter in a fine stream, whisk constantly, blend in 1/4 juice of a lemon along with salt and pepper to taste.

My photo/08

28

Apple Pancake

Core, but don't peel 1 apple, cut into 12 slices. In a heavy skillet melt 5 tb. butter, stir in 1/4 tsp. cinnamon, 1/4 tsp. nutmeg and 2 tb. sugar. Add apple slices and saute until tender. Mix 1 cup Bisquick with 2/3 cup milk, 1 beaten egg and 1 tb. sugar just until flour has moistened. Pour over apples slices on low heat and cook for 10 minutes or until no longer shinny. Place under boiler until lightly browned. Drop upside down on a plate. Serve with syrup and butter.

29

apple Wheatena

Melt 3 tb. butter in a heavy medium pot, add 1 tsp. salt, 1/2 tsp ground coriander and 1/4 ground cumin, mix together for 20 to 30 seconds. Add 4 cups apple juice and bring to a boil. Whisk in 1 cup wheatena, then lower heat, cover and leave for 5 minutes before serving.

30

My photo/08

Tomato and Cheese Souffle

Melt 2 tb. butter add 3 tb. flour, stir until smooth. Then add 3/4 cup hot milk, cook until thickened, stir in 1/2 cup can tomato soup, 1 1/2 cup grated cheese and heat until cheese has melted, remove from heat and add 1/4 tsp. dry mustard, 4 egg yolks 1 at a time beating to mix in well. Beat the egg whites until stiff, but not dry. Fold into mixture. Pour into a well greased baking dish. Place in a pan of water while baking at 350 for 50 to 60 minutes or until firm.

31

Garrys Photo/08

Banana Omelet

Beat 4 eggs lightly, add 2 tb. light cream along with 2 mashed bananas and 1 tb. brown sugar with a pinch of salt. Fry on a medium low heat until set. Fold and turn onto a platter. Sprinkle with powdered sugar. Serves 6.

32

My Photo/07

Spanish Omelet

Brown 4 slices of minced bacon, add 1 diced tomato, 1 diced onion, 1 diced small green pepper, cook on medium low heat slowly for 10 to 15 minutes, stir occasionally. Beat 6 eggs with 3 tb. milk, add 1/2 tsp. salt and 1/4 tsp. pepper. Melt 1 tb. butter in a heavy skillet and pour in egg mixture, frying slowly, until eggs are set. Pour bacon, green pepper, tomato mixture over cooked eggs, fold omelet and turn onto a platter. Sprinkle with cheese of choice, cover until cheese has melted. Serves 6

Nic's Photo/07

Yam Biscuits

Combine 1 cup of cooked and mashed yams with 1/4 cup butter, 1 beaten egg, stir in 1 cup sifted flour, 1/2 tsp. salt and 2 tsp. baking powder blend well into yam mixture. Drop dough in around the edge of a casserole by a tb. spoon full, in your favorite casserole dish. Bake at 350 for 30 minutes.

My photos/ Nics graphics/ 08

Pancake Bulk Mix

Mix 10 cup whole wheat flour, 10 cups white flour, 3 cups powdered milk, 3/4 cup baking powder, 1/4 cup salt, 2 tb baking soda.

When using add 1 egg, 2 to 3 tb. for 1 cup mix and just enough water to make a thick batter but still thin enough to pour from a 1/4 cup on a hot grill. Cook until bubbles form and flip to brown on each side.

Garry's photo/My graphics/08

Morning Oat Cakes

The night before mix together 2 1/4 cups rolled oats, 1 tsp salt, with 2 cups butter milk to make like a batter consistency. Cover and let stand over night.   In the morning add 2 eggs and beat well, combine in 4 to 6 tb. oil and 1 tsp soda mixed with a few spoons of hot water to dissolve, beat to mix in, should have the consistency of thick cream, may need to add more cream or water.   Pour from a 1/4 cup and cook on medium heat in a heavy frying pan, when bubbles form flip and brown on the other side. Serve with syrup with a side of bacon.   *My photo/07*

Egg Balls

Mash 6 hard cooked egg yolks, 1 1/2 tb. melted butter, 1 beaten egg, 1 tsp. salt and 1/4 tsp. pepper mix to a smooth paste. Form into little balls, roll in bread crumbs. Saute in 2 tb. oil until browned. Serves 6.

Nics

37

Hungry Style Breakfast

Scrub 2 medium potatoes and cut into chunks, cut 1/2 lb. bacon into 1 inch pieces, fry in a heavy skillet until crisp. Add 1 small chopped onion along with potatoes salt and pepper to taste, cook on medium heat stir to browned and crisp. Drop heat to low, make a nest in 4 spots in potato mixture and drop a egg into each, salt and pepper and cover and cook until eggs are cooked to likeness. Serve with toast.

38

Garry's photo/08

Morning oat Muffins

Mix 2 cups rolled oats, 3/4 cup melted butter and 1 1/2 cups milk, mix well let stand over night. In the morning add 1/2 cup brown sugar, 1 well beaten egg, 1 cup flour, 1/2 cup raisins and 1 cup chopped walnuts. Spoon into a well greased muffin tin with a tb. spoon 3/4 full and bake in a 350 oven for 20 to 25 minutes or until done. Makes 16 to 18 muffins.

Oven Baked Fruit French toast

Foamy Fruit Sauce

Thicken any canned fruit of berries, cherries, plums or what ever choice. Mix 2 tsp. corn starch and 2 tb. sugar for each cup of syrup and cook over direct heat.

Cut 6 slices of texas bread diagonal, arrange in a greased casserole dish over lapping. Pour a mixture of 3 beaten eggs with 1/2 cup milk and 1 tsp. vanilla, set aside for 10 minutes. Bake in a 350 oven until golden brown.

Stir constantly until thickened. Add 1 tsp lemon juice and fold in 1 beaten egg white.

Garry's photo/06

Madeleines

Mix 1 1/4 cup sugar, 4 eggs 1 tb. orange rind. Add 1 1/4 cup flour and 1 tsp. baking powder a little at a time with 1 cup melted butter just enough to incorporate, mix in 1 tsp. vanilla. Pour into a muffin tin and bake at 350 for 25 to 30 minutes.

Garry's Photo

Morning Scramble

Combine 5 beaten eggs add 1 cup milk in a large bowl and beat well. Add 5 slices of cubed bread, 1 cup cooked cubed ham, 1 cup shredded cheddar cheese, 2 to 3 sliced large mushrooms, 1/2 cup chopped green pepper, 1/4 cup chopped onion, 3/4 tsp. season salt, 1/4 tsp. dry mustard, salt and pepper to taste, mix well. Pour into a baking dish and let stand for 10 minutes. Bake 350 for 45 to 50 minutes, or until set. Serve with toast.

42

Garry's Photo

Brunch

My photos/08

43

Mini Quiche

In a bowl mix 1 cup chopped ham, 2 to 3 green onions chopped, 1 medium chopped tomato and 1/4 chopped green pepper along with 6 beaten eggs, salt and pepper to taste. Add 1/3 cup milk stir to mix well. Pour into a large greased muffin tin. Sprinkle with cheddar cheese, half way through baking. Bake in a 350 oven until set about 15 to 25 minutes. serve on top of toast.

My photos/07

Garry's birds/07

44

Carrot Cashew Curried Soup

In a large pot add 8 cups of water, mix in 1 tsp. crushed garlic, 1 tsp. ginger, 1 tsp. dry mustard, 1 tsp. cumin, 1 tsp. coriander, 1 tsp. dill weed, 1 tsp. turmeric, 1 tsp. curry powder, 1 cup brown rice, 3 cups finely diced carrots, 1/2 cup diced onions and 2 cups diced potatoes, Cook until all is tender. Then add 1/4 cup chopped parsley and 1/2 cup cashew nuts. Serve when still hot.

My photo/07

Parmesan Confetti Dip

Mix together, 1 cup sour cream, 1/2 cup grated Parmesan cheese, 1/2 cup salad dressing, 1/2 cup of finely chopped green and red pepper, 1/2 cup finely chopped green onion, 1/2 tsp. garlic powder. Mix well to incorporate and chill for 1 to 2 hours before serving. Serve with crackers, bread rounds or chips.

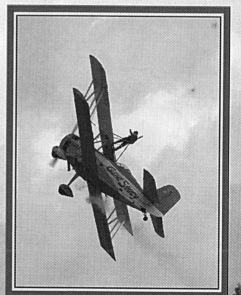

46

Barley Casserole

Melt 1/2 cup margarine in a skillet, add 1 cup chopped onions, cook onions add fresh trimmed sliced mushrooms, cook over medium heat until tender. Add 1 1/2 cup pearl barley and cook until delicately browned. Turn into a casserole, add 4 oz. pimento, 1/4 tsp. salt and pepper, mix in to distribute. Mix in 3 cups chicken bouillon. Bake in a 350 oven for 1 hour our until barley has cooked through and tender.

My Photos/06

French Onion Soup

Slice 4 large onions and cook in 2 tb. margarine until golden brown. Add 6 cups water along with 3 tb. chicken soup base. Simmer for 15 to 20 minutes. Pour into 4 oven proof soup bowls. Top each with a lightly toasted slice of French bread sprinkle with grated nippy cheese. Just before serving place under a broiler to partially melt cheese.

48

My photos/07

Vegetable Soup

Saute 1/2 cup melted margurine, 1/2 cup diced celery, 1/2 cup diced carrots, 1/2 cup diced turnips and 1/2 cup diced onion. Add 3 cups water cook over medium heat for 10 to 15 minutes. Add 1/2 cup peas, 1/2 cup corn and simmer 10 more minutes. Then add 1 tsp. basil, 1 tb chicken powder base, salt and pepper to taste, serve hot.

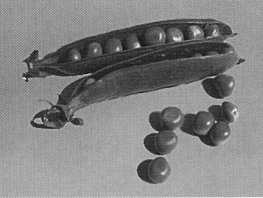

Garry's photo/08

Egg Casserole

Melt 1/4 cup butter stir in 1/4 cup flour until smooth, Gradually add 2 1/2 cups milk stirring constantly add 1/4 tsp. thyme, marjoram and 1 lb. grated cheddar cheese, stirring until cheese melts. In a large greased casserole dish make layers of 2 dozen hard boiled sliced eggs, 1 lb. bacon, fried and crumbled add the cheese sauce and 1/4 cup snipped parsley on top. Bake in a preheated oven at 350 and bake for 30 minutes. Serve with toast or English muffins. serves 8 to 10.

My Photo/07

Tossed Foo Yung Salad

In a salad bowl combine 1 medium head lettuce cut into bite size pieces. Add 2 cups canned, drained bean sprouts, 1 cup canned sliced and drained water chestnuts. 5 slices cooked crisp and crumbled bacon, add 2 hard cooked, sliced eggs.   Dressing...... Combine 1 cup salad oil, 1/2 cup sugar, 1/2 cup ketchup, 1/4 cup vinegar, 2 tb. grated onion and 2 tsp. Worcestershire sauce. Shake in a screw top jar and shake until well mixed. Add to salad just before serving, toss lightly.

My photos Nics blue bird/08

51

Fresh Cream of Tomato Soup

Wash 6 to 8 fresh ripe and sliced tomatoes, Combine with 1/2 cup chopped celery, 2 to 3 tb. chopped onion, 2 tsp. sugar and 1/4 tsp. pepper, simmer slowly for 20 to 25 minutes or until soft, press through a sieve approx. 3 1/2 cups. In a medium sauce pan melt 4 tb. margarine add 4 tb. flour, stir until smooth gradually add tomato pulp. Cook over low heat stirring constantly until thickened. Just before serving add 3 cups milk, stir well and heat over low heat.

My photo/ Garrys ladybug

Red Flannel Hash

Mix together 1 cup cooked chopped corned beef. Add 1 small minced onion, 1/2 tsp. salt, 1/8 tsp. pepper and 1 tsp. worcestershire sauce. Melt 1 to 2 tb. bacon fat or margarine in a large frying pan, add 1 cup cold chopped potatoes and spread out evenly in pan. Brown slowly, when a crust has formed, turn as a pan cake and brown the other side.

My Photos/ 07 Garrys Bird

53

Vichyssoise

Dissolve 2 chicken bouillon cubes in 2 cups boiling water. Saute 1 small sliced onion in 2 tb. butter until tender and golden brown. Add 2 medium size peeled and sliced potatoes and onion to broth, simmer until potatoes are tender. pour into a coarse sieve. Add 1/2 tsp. salt, 1/8 tsp. pepper and 1/8 tsp. nutmeg. Chill for several hours. Just before serving stir in 1/2 cup cream. Serve cold with chopped green onion on top of each serving. serves 4.

Garrys Photo/06

Mexican Fiesta

Cook 1 lb. ground beef stir until browned, drain fat. Season with salt and pepper, set aside. In a bowl mix 1 cups shredded cheese, 1 cup sour cream, 2/3 cup mayo and 2 tb. chopped onion set aside. Mix 2 cups biscuit mix with 1/2 cup water until dough forms, with floured hands pat dough onto a greased baking sheet pressing 1/2 inch up the sides. Layer meat and add 2 chopped tomatoes, 3/4 cup chopped green pepper, spoon on sour cream mixture. Bake at 350 oven for 20 to 30 minutes

55

My Photos/08

Fruity Fritters

Sift 1 cup flour and 1/2 tsp. salt, pinch of cinnamon and nutmeg in to a large bowl. Beat 1 egg, add 1 1/4 cup milk. Pour in the flour mixture and beat well. Add 1 1/2 tb melted butter. Fold in 1/4 cup chopped raisins, 1/4 cup currants. 1 1/2 cup chopped glazed cherries and 1 1/2 tb. citron. Set for 1 hour. Pour 2 tb. batter into a hot greased fry pan, turn when dry. and cook the other side.

56

My Photos/ 08

Basic Crepe Batter

Beat 2 eggs with 1 1/4 cup milk, in a bowl sift 1 cup flour, 1/4 tsp. salt, add to the egg and milk mixture. Mix in 2 tb. butter with a whisk and blend thoroughly until smooth. Strain to remove any lumps, set for 1 hour, add milk if needed. Pour 1 to 2 tbs. of batter in the center of a hot, lightly oiled frying pan. Tilt to spread the batter to the edges of pan, cook until top is dry, turn over and cook the other side for 15 seconds. Makes 12 crepes.

Crepes Suzette

Cream together 2/3 cup butter, 5 tbs. sugar, 1 1/2 tb grated orange rind, 1 tsp. grated lemon rind, place mixture into a large frying pan, heat until melted, stirring constantly. Add 1/2 cup orange juice, 1 1/2 tb. lemon juice and Grand Marnier and mix well, cook until thickens. Place crepes one by one into the sauce, when soaked fold into quarters set on platter. Heat sauce slightly and pour over creps

Ignite and serve when the flame has gone out.

— My Photos/ 08

57

Horseradish Lime Molds

1 pkg. lime jelly powder add 1 1/2 cup boiled water, stir to dissolve. Add 2 tb. cider vineger, 2 tb. lemon juice, and 1 tsp. horseradish, refrigerate. When partially thickened fold in 2 tb. chopped sweet pickles, 1/2 cup finely shredded cabbage and 1/2 cup grated carrots. Turn into a small mold that has been cooled.   Serve when set.   58   *My photo/08*

Potato Doughnuts

Cook 8 medium potatoes. Drain and save water. Mash and measure 2 cups. Add 1 cup flour to potatoes to make a firm dough. Dissolve 4 tb. yeast and 1 tsp. sugar in 1 cup warm water. Mix mashed potatoes, potato water, 4 well beaten eggs, 1 tsp. salt, 1 cup sugar and 1 cup vegetable oil, add to yeast mixture. Add 15 cups flour 2 cups at a time to make a firm yet soft dough. Let rise to double size, punch down, let rise again, punch down and roll out to 1/2 thick, cut with a doughnut cutter, rise again until double size. Fry in oil until brown. dust with icing sugar.

59

Farmers Plate Salad

Mix 1 cup finely chopped celery, 2 cups shredded cabbage, 2 tb. finely chopped onion, 1 cup cubed chicken or ham, salt and pepper to taste. Add 1/2 cup salad dressing, 2 tb sour cream, with 2 tb vineger and mix well.

My photo/08

Egg and Nut Crepes

Mix together 1 cup mayonnaise, 1 1/2 tsp. salt, 1 tsp. coriander, 1/4 tsp. pepper, 1/8 tsp. paprika, 1/2 tsp. dry mustard in a blender. Pour the mixture on to 10 chopped hard boiled eggs, mix with 1 cup chopped nuts, 1 cup chopped celery and 2 minced scallions. Fill each crepe with the mixture and fold over and place in a greased shallow baking dish. Melt 3 tb. butter in a sauce pan. Remove from heat and stir in 2 tb. flour until smooth. Return to a low heat and cook for 2 minutes. Add 1 tsp. dry mustard, 1/2 tsp salt, 1/8 tsp cayenne pepper and 1/2 tsp paprika, mix well. Slowly add 2 cups milk, stirring constantly. Cook until thickened. Remove from heat. Add 1 cup grated cheddar cheese stir until cheese has melted. Pour the sauce over crepes and bake in a 350 oven for 15 minutes.

My photo/07

61

Pan Potato Scones

Mash 1/2 cup cooked potatoes, no butter or milk. In another bowl sift 1/4 cup self raising flour and 2 tb. margarine, mix with hands just enough to incorporate. Add potato, 1 to 2 tb. sugar and dried cranberries blend thoroughly. Apply just enough milk to make a firm rolling consistency to form into a round greased frying pan. Cook on medium high heat until batter has a golden brown, approximately 3 minutes. Flip to brown the other side, serve hot.

My Photo/08

Desserts

My Photo/Graphics

Daiquiri Pie

Beat 8 oz. pkg. soften cream cheese until light and fluffy. Add 14 oz. can sweetened condensed milk, 6 oz. can frozen concentrate limeade thawed, beat until smooth. Add 1/3 cup light rum and a few drops of food coloring. Fold in 4 oz. frozen whipped topping. Pour into a 9 in. graham cracker crust and refrigerate 6 to 8 hour. Garnish with slices of lime.

Garrys Photos/06

Sweet Potato Pudding

Combine 3 cups grated raw sweet potato, 1/2 cup sugar, 1/2 cup maple sirup, 1 cup milk 1 tsp. nutmeg, 2 tb. melted butter, 1/2 cup chopped nuts and 1/2 tsp. salt. Add 2 well beaten eggs and pour into a buttered shallow pan. Bake in a moderately hot oven at 375 for 50 to 60 minutes. Serves 6.

My photos/06

Peach Cobbler

Empty 2 1/2 cups canned sliced peaches into a shallow baking dish. Add 2 tb. granulated tapioca, let stand for 10 minutes. Add 1/4 cup sugar, 1/4 tsp. salt and 1/4 tsp. cinnamon, dash of nutmeg mix well, dot with 1 tb. butter. Roll out a biscuit dough to a thickness of 1/4 inch thick. Arrange over the top of the peach mixture, bake in a hot oven at 400 for 30 minutes or until golden brown.

My Photo/06

Apple Crow's Nest

Arrange 4 tart cored and peeled apples in a greased pie tin and dot with butter. Sprinkle with 3/4 cup sugar mixed with 2 1/2 tsp. cinnamon and 3 tb. chopped nuts. Sift 1 cup flour, 2 tsp. baking powder 1/4 tsp. salt and 1/4 cup sugar together twice. Cut in 3 tb. margarine add 1/4 cup milk gradually to make a soft dough. Spread over apples. Bake in a hot oven at 400 until apples are tender, about 25 minutes. Turn out upside down, serve hot with whipped cream.

67

Tina's Sour cream Coffee Cake

In a small bowl mix 2 beaten eggs with 1/4 cup brown sugar and 1/4 cup of splenda. In a measuring cup mix 3/4 cup low fat sour cream along with 1/4 cup water and mix well, mix into egg mixture.

In a large bowl mix 1 1/2 cup flour, 2 tsp. baking powder, 1 tsp. salt, 1 tsp. cinnamon, 1 cup rolled oats, mix together well. Make a well in the flour mixture and add egg mixture, mix just to incorporate, pour into a greased and floured cake pan. For a crumb topping mix 1/2 cup rolled oats, 1 tsp cinnamon, 1/4 tsp. nutmeg, 1/4 cup chopped walnuts and 2 tb. tub margarine and mix with hands until crumbly, top on cake in pan. Bake at 375 for 35

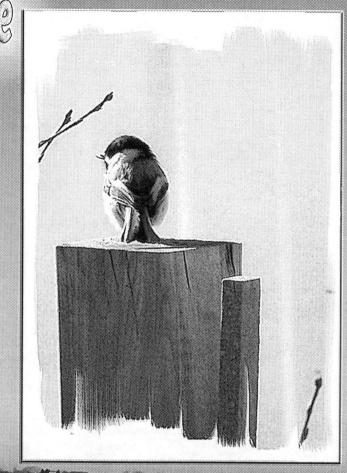

68

Garrys bird/ my photo/08

Rhubarb Cream Pie

Blend 1 1/2 cup sugar, 3 tb. flour, 1 tsp. nutmeg and 1 1/2 tb. butter. Add 2 well beaten eggs until smooth. Pour over 3 cups cubed rhubarb in a pastry lined pie pan. Top with pastry. Bake in a 450 oven for 10 minutes. Then drop temperature to 350 for 30 minutes.

My photos/ 08

69

Grape and Tomato Pie

Slice 3 firm tomatoes thin and place a layer in a pie shell sprinkled with part of 1 1/4 cup sugar mixed with 3 tb. flour, cut 1 1/2 cup concord grapes all most in half and remove any seeds and lay open over tomatoes, cover with 1/2 of the sugar, flour mixture with a sprinkle of salt, repeat layers. Cover with top crust, wet edges to stick, press to seal, trim. Brush with water and bake 450 for 10 min. set at 350 and bake at 350 for 30 min. or until well browned. 70

My photo/ 07

Garrys ducks

Strawberry Cheese Parfait

Whip 1 cup whipping cream until thick. Beat 1 egg white until stiff. Add 1 1/2 cup cottage cheese to 1/2 tsp. salt, 1 tsp. vanilla, 2 tb. sugar, beat until smooth. Fold egg white and whipped cream into cottage cheese gently until well mixed. Alternate spoonfuls of the cheese mixture with 2 pkg. of frozen thawed strawberries into parfait glasses. Chill for 1 to 2 hours before serving. Serves 6 to 8.

71

Garry's Photo/08

Queens Pudding

Sift 1 cup flour, 1 tsp. baking powder and salt to taste. Add 1/2 cup sugar, mix well. Add 1/2 cup raisins, 1/2 cup milk and 2 tb. melted butter to dry ingredients. Place batter mixture into a greased casserole. Combine 1 cup brown sugar, 1 tb. butter, 1 tsp. vanilla along with 2 cups boiling water mix just to combine and pour over the batter. Bake in a 325 oven for 40 minutes. serves 6 .

Nicks dragon flys
Nics photo/ 07
Cins frog/ 07

Rice Pudding Custard

Cook 1 cup rice. Add 1 qt. milk, 4 beaten eggs, 1 cup sugar and 1 cup raisins. Pour into a greased baking dish. Sprinkle with cinnamon. Bake in a 300 oven for 30 minutes.

My photo/ 07
Nic's yard

Apple Blossoms

Sift 2 1/4 cups flour twice with 1 tsp. baking powder, 1/2 tsp. salt. In another bowl cream 8 tbs shortening with 2 1/2 cups sugar, add 1 beaten egg and beat well, then beat in 1 tsp. vanilla and 1 tb. cream of tarter. Add to dry ingredients a little at a time and combine well, wrap in plastic wrap and chill for 3 to 4 hours or over night. Turn out dough on a floured board and roll out 1/8 inch thick. Cut out 2 inch rounds with a cutter. Arrange on greased cookie sheets. Bake in a preheated oven at 350 for 10 minutes.

Combine in a sauce pan 1 box jelly powder, with 1/2 cup boiling water, stir to dissolve, keep warm. In a double boiler add 2 egg whites with 1 1/2 cups sugar, 5 tb. water, 1 tb. corn syrup and 1 tsp. salt. Cook and beat with beater for 7 minutes. Stir in jelly mixture, beat to blend, cool until thickened. Drop 1/4 tsp. on the centre of each cookie. Top with pink mellow and dip in coconut. Makes 3 dozen cookies.

My photo/07

Low Cal Peanut Butter Cookies

Sift together 2/3 cup flour, 1/2 tsp. baking soda, 1/2 tsp. baking powder, 1/4 tsp. salt. Combine 6 tb. peanut butter and 2 eggs. Add 1/2 cup equal sugar and mix well. Thoroughly mix in dry ingredients. Drop by a tsp. full onto a greased cookie sheet, flatten with a water dipped fork. Bake in a preheated oven at 375 for 10 to 12 minutes or until done. Makes 32 cookies. 1 cookie 40 calories.

75

Garry's Photo/07

Berry Slump

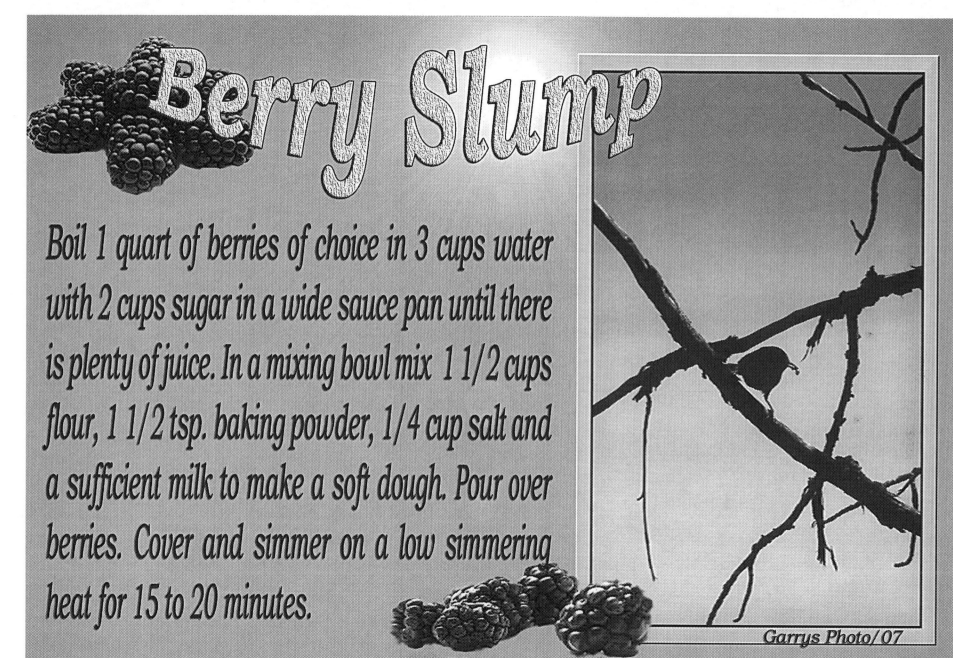

Boil 1 quart of berries of choice in 3 cups water with 2 cups sugar in a wide sauce pan until there is plenty of juice. In a mixing bowl mix 1 1/2 cups flour, 1 1/2 tsp. baking powder, 1/4 cup salt and a sufficient milk to make a soft dough. Pour over berries. Cover and simmer on a low simmering heat for 15 to 20 minutes.

Garrys Photo/07

76

Grape Sherbet

Boil 3 cups water and 1 1/2 cups sugar together for 10 minutes add 2 cups grape juice and the juice from 1 lemon, cool and freeze. When partly frozen fold in 1 egg white stiffly beaten, continue freezing.

Nic's

Nic's

77

Gurrys photo/07

Vanilla Ice Cream

Scald 1 1/2 cups milk. Separate 2 eggs. Beat yolks and add 1/2 cup sugar and 1 tb. cornstarch. Combine mixture to milk, cook in a double boiler for 20 to 25 minutes, stirring occasionally. Cool. Beat egg whites until stiff. Add 1/8 tsp. salt and fold in to cooked mixture, add 2 tsp. vanilla. Pour into a freezing tray and chill to a heavy mush. Beat until fluffy. Whip 1 cup whipping cream and fold into mixture, return to tray and freeze.

78

Frozen Pudding

Mix 1 1/2 cups orange juice, 1/4 cup lemon juice, add 1/2 cup sugar and dissolve. Beat 2 cup cream until thick add the fruit juices, 1/3 cup powdered sugar and 2 tsp. vanilla. Stir in 1/2 cup raisins, 1/2 cup chopped maraschino cherries and 1/2 cup chopped walnuts, chill to freeze.

79

My photo/08

Carrot Pie

Peel and cook 2 lb. carrots, mashed finely, mix 4 eggs into mashed carrots add 2 cups milk, 2 cups brown sugar, 1 tsp. cinnamon, salt and ginger. Line 2 large pie pans with pastery. Pour in carrot mixture and bake at 400 for 45 minutes or until baked threw. Serve with ice cream.

My photo/ 07

Party Plum Pudding

Cream 1 tb. butter with 1/2 cup sugar and 1/2 cup brown sugar. Sift together 2 1/2 cup flour, 2 tsp. baking powder, 1 tsp. salt, 1/2 tsp. cinnamom, 1/2 tsp. cloves, 1/2 tsp. allspice and 1/4 tsp. nutmeg. Now add together 1 cup butter milk with 3/4 tsp. soda mixed in, add to cream mixture alternately with dry ingredients. Add 1 cup dates. Place in a greased pudding pan and steam for 2 hours. Serves 8 to 10.

81

Garry's Photo/08

Crumble Apple Grape Pie

Wash and stem 3 cups of concord grapes. Slip skins from grapes and set skins aside. Combine 1 1/2 cups cut up apples with grape pulp. Simmer gently until soft, press through sieve to remove seeds and apple skins. Stir in 1 tb. quick tapioca, 1 cup sugar, 2 tsp. lemon juice and grape skins into the pulp. Pour into uncooked pie shell. Sprinkle with a crumb topping. Bake at 450 for 10 minutes, reduce heat to 350, bake for 25 minutes.

Crumb Topping........

Mix together 3/4 cup brown sugar with 3/4 cup flour. Blend in 5 tb soft butter until crumbly.

82

My Photo/07

Garry's skunk/08

Richmond Maids of Honour

In a double boiler cook 1 cup of sweet milk, 1 cup butter milk until it curds, then strain. Rub the curd through a sieve. Beat 1 cup sugar, pinch of salt and 4 egg yolks together. Add juice from 1 lemon and rind, add the curd and mix lightly. Fill little pastry shells of puff pastry with a large spoonful into each shell and bake at 350 for 15 to 20 minutes. Do not remove until cold.

My photo/ graphics/ 07

83

They're all coming for Dinner

Garrys Photo
My Graphics

84a

Fruit Compote

Slice 1 can peaches and pears with juice, 1 can pineapple tidbits with juice, 1 can orange segments, drained and 20 to 24 maraschino cherries, drained. Place all fruit in a medium size sauce pan, add 3/4 cup packed brown sugar and 1 tsp. curry powder, bring to a boil. Mix 3 tb. corn starch with 1/4 cup water, pour into boiling fruit stirring constantly until boiling starts again and thickens. Serve over ice cream or pound cake. to reheat, in a 350 oven for 30 minutes until bubbly for a even and smooth saucy fruit.

Oven Fried Potatoes

Wash and peel 6 cups thinly sliced potatoes. Slice 2 medium onions. Layer potatoes and onions in a buttered baking dish. Heat 1/2 cup butter on low heat, add 1 tsp. salt and pepper. Pour melted butter over potatoes and toss. Bake in a 350 oven for 1 1/2 hour, toss occasionally to brown evenly.

85   Garry's Photo/08

Delmonico Potatoes

Heat 9 cups water to a boiling in a large pan, add 1 tsp salt and 1 8oz pkg. dehydrated sliced potatoes lower heat and cover, cook for 20 minutes. As potatoes cook, combine 1 can of 10 oz. chicken gravy, 1 tb. grated onion, 1 tsp. dry mustard, 1 tsp. paprika and 1/4 tsp. pepper in 1 1/4 cup milk gradually. Drain potatoes and place in a baking dish, sprinkle with cheese and pimientos, toss to mix, cover with gravy mixture evenly, cover with foil. Bake in a 350 oven for 45 minutes or until bubbly hot and cheese has melted.

86

My Photo/07

Vichissoise Potato Leek Soup

Saute 3 peeled, cleaned and chopped leeks whites only, until soft in 2 tb. butter and 2 tb. olive oil. Add 4 peeled and chopped potatoes with 6 cups chicken stock, bring to a boil and skim. Add several sprigs thyme, tied together, simmer until vegetables are soft, cool. Remove thyme. Puree soup with a hand blender and chill well. Blend in 1 cup cream until frothy, season with salt and pepper to taste. Serve cold and garnish with chives.

My Photo/08

Two Potato Bake

Grease a baking dish with a blend of 2 cloves of peeled mashed garlic with 2 tb. of room temperature butter. Slice paper thin 4 to 5 potatoes and the same with sweet potatoes. Alternate potatoes, salt and pepper each layer, blend each color on top to vary the color. In a bowl mix 3 lightly beaten eggs with 2 cups milk or cream and 1 tsp. nutmeg. Pour evenly and slowly over top. Bake in a 450 oven for 30 minutes, reduce heat and bake at 350 for 1 hour.

My Photos/07

Kathy's Baked Hash Browns

Shred 3 cups of cheddar cheese, set a side . Mix 4 cups of hash browns with 2 cans of cream of chicken soup, 1 cup shredded cheese, mix well, turn into a greased baking dish, sprinkle remaining cheese bake in a 350 oven for 1 hour, serve hot.

Garry's Photo/07

89

Country Browned Hash

Mix 1 cup cooked minced cornbeef, 1 tsp. grated onion, 1 tsp. salt and pepper, 2 cups mashed potatoes, 1 egg and just enough beef stock to hold mixture together. Heat a heavy fry pan along with 1/2 tsp. cooking oil. Spread mixture evenly in frying pan and reduce heat, cook slowly to brown evenly. Top with a plate and flip frying pan to drop on plate with browned side on up, cut into wedges and serve hot.

90

My Graphics

Potato Julienne

Clean and trim 4 large celery stalks and peel 4 medium potatoes, cut into julienne strips 1/8" thick x 2" long. Keep potatoes in cold water to stop browning. Heat 2 tb. butter, add celery and 1 small finely chopped onion. Saute 4 to 5 minutes. Drain potatoes and dry in a cloth. Place into celery and onion mixture, add salt and pepper, stir to blend. Cover and cook until tender, stirring occasionally, approximately 10 minutes. Dust with chopped parsley.

91

Scalloped Cabbage and Celery

Shred 1 small head cabbage and 1 small cluster of diced celery cook just until tender. In a sauce pan melt 2 tb. butter mix in 2 tb. flour gradually until smooth, add vegetable stock from cooked cabbage, little at a time stirring until smooth and thickened, season to taste. Place vegetables into a greased casserole dish. Pour the sauce over evenly. Crisp up 4 diced bacon slices, top with 2 cups cubed bread crumbs mixed with the bacon top over the cabbage mixture. Bake in a 350 oven until browned.

92

My Photo/07

Scalloped Corn

Beat 2 eggs in a medium bowl, add 1 can cream of corn, 2 tb. flour, 1 tb. sugar and 1 tb. butter, mix to blend until flour has mixed in. Add 3/4 cup milk, 1 tsp. salt, 1/8 tsp pepper and 1 tsp. dry onion flakes, mix and pour into a greased casserole dish. In a sauce pan melt 1 tb. butter, stir in 1/2 cup bread crumbs. Sprinkle over corn mixture evenly. Bake in a 350 oven for 1 hour or until set and golden brown.

My Photo/08

Broccoli and Oranges

Cut 1 bunch broccoli into flowerets. Heat 1 tb. oil in skillet on medium heat. Add 2 minced shallots and cook stirring until tender about 2 minutes. Add broccoli and cook and stir until cooked but still crisp, add 2 oranges sectioned and season with salt and pepper along with 1 pinch of cayenne. Serve hot.

Jewish Sweet Sour Beans

Heat 2 tb. cooking oil, add 2 tb. flour, stir until smooth. Add 1 tb. brown sugar, 1/4 tsp. salt, 1 1/2 tb. vinegar, 1/8 tsp cinnamon and 2 1/2 cups cooked green beans. Cover and simmer until liquid has reduced .

My Photo/08

Spicy Red Cabbage

Cook 2 1/2 lb. shredded red cabbage, 1 red apple cored, peeled, and quartered, 1 thinly sliced onion, 2 bay leaves, salt and pepper. Add 1/2 cup water in a covered stainless steel or enameled pot over moderately high heat. Stir occasionally for 10 minutes or until cabbage is tender, discard the bay leaves. Stir in 1/2 cup sherry and 1 1/2 cup vinegar, serve hot.

95

My Photos/08

Carrots and Zucchini with Pine Nut Rice

Combine 1/2 cup long grain rice with 1 cup water and bring to a boil. Reduce heat, cover and cook over low heat for about 18 minutes, until all water has been absorbed leaving a tender rice. Coarsely chop 1 1/4 cup onion, 1 1/2 cup carrots, 2 1/3 cup zucchini and 1 cup sliced mushrooms. Saute vegetables in 2 tb. hot oil for 10 minutes add rice, season with salt and pepper, mix in 3 tb. pine nuts.

96

Garrys Photos

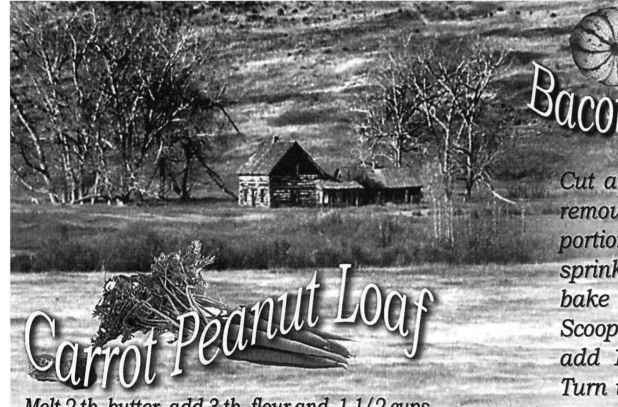

Bacon Baked Squash

Cut a 3 lb. squash in pieces and remove seeds and the stringy portions. Brush with butter, sprinkle with salt and pepper, bake in a 350 oven until tender. Scoop from the shell, mash and add 1/2 cup milk, salt to taste. Turn into a buttered baking dish. Fry 1 cup diced bacon until crisp, drain and sprinkle on top of squash. Bake for 20 to 30 minutes.

Carrot Peanut Loaf

Melt 2 tb. butter, add 3 tb. flour and 1 1/2 cups stewed tomatoes. Cook and stir constantly, until thickened. Add 2 cups roasted chopped peanuts, 2 cups finely chopped carrots, 1 cup dry bread crumbs, 1/4 cup chopped parsley, 1 beaten egg, 1 tsp. salt and 1/8 tsp. pepper. Mix thoroughly. Mold into a loaf. Line a greased loaf pan with wax paper. Pack in the mixture and bake in a 400 oven for 1 hour.

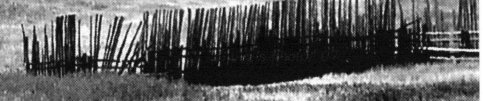

Garry's Photo/07

Taco Salad

Heat 2 cups ground beef mix with 1 cup green chili peppers for a hot dish ? Combine 1 head lettuce torn into bite size pieces. 3 chopped tomatoes, 1 large chopped avocado, 3 chopped green onions, 1 1/2 cups grated cheddar cheese, 1 can drained kidney beans in a large salad bowl, add ground beef mixture and toss. Add tortilla chips and salad dressing of choice.

98

My Photo/08

Roasted Lentil Loaf

Soak 8 oz. lentils over night in cold water. In the same water cook on a medium hot, boil until the water has absorbed, beat until smooth. Heat 2 oz. vegetable oil fry 2 chopped onions, 2 large skinned tomatoes and 1 small peeled, cored and chopped apple until soft, add the lentils, along with 1 tsp. sage and 2 oz. bread crumbs. Mix in 1 beaten egg, press into a greased loaf pan and cover with greased paper. Bake in a 375 oven for 1 hour and 45 minutes to 2 hour. Serve in a brown gravy.

Nut Cutlets

Chopped 8 oz. peanuts. Heat 2 oz. vegetable oil and fry 2 chopped onions, 2 large skinned tomatoes and 1 small peeled, cored and chopped apple until soft. Add the peanuts, 1 oz. oat meal or bread crumbs with 1 tsp. sage and seasoning, mix in 1 beaten egg and just enough milk to give a fairly moist consistency, form into cutlets brush with egg, dip in bread crumbs, fry or bake in 375 oven for 15 to 20 minutes or until crisp and browned.

Cindy's Photo/07

Tina's Tomato Macaroni Soup

Cook 2 cups macararoni according to package directions. While cooking brown 1/2 lb. ground beef. Chop 1/2 cup onion, 1/2 cup chop celery, 1 can stewed tomatoes cut in chunks while in can, add to ground beef and stir in to salute until tender, add to cooked macaroni along with 1 can of tomato soup with 1 tsp. salt, pepper and 1 tb. chicken broth simmer for 10 more minutes.

My photo/ 08

Oriental Meatballs

Mix 1 1/2 lbs. ground beef, 1 egg, 1/4 tsp. ginger and 1 tsp salt, 1/8 pepper for meat balls, shaped into 1 1/4 balls. Fry in 2 tb. oil until browned on all sides remove and keep warm. Saute 1/2 cup chopped onion, 1 cup sliced celery until onions are transparent. Add 1 cup beef bouillon, 1 tb. soy sauce, 1/2 tsp ginger, 2 tb. sugar,1/4 cup vinegar and 2 tb cornstarch, mix to combine. Add 1 can peaches and meatballs, simmer covered for 10 minutes. Serve

101

Garry's photo/07

China Hash

Brown 1 lb. ground beef in a frying pan add 1 chopped green pepper, 1/2 cup chopped celery, 1 cup chopped onion, mix and stir to break up meat and cook through. In a small pot boil 1 cup water and dissolve 3 beef bouillon cubes, pour into meat mixture. Add 1 can drained sliced mushrooms, 1/2 cup long grain rice, 1 can drained water chest nuts, 1 can drained bamboo shoots, 2 cups bean sprouts, 3 tb. soy sauce, 1 tsp. salt, and 1/4 tsp pepper mix lightly turn into a greased casserole dish cover and bake in a 350 oven for 45 minutes or until rice has cooked.

102

My photo/08

oriental Chicken

Cut chicken from 1 whole cooked chicken coarsely. Saute 4 oz. cooked wild rice in 6 tb. olive oil until crisp, drain on paper towels. Toss chicken with rice, 3 tb. peanut oil and sesame oil. Mix in 1/4 lb. steamed snow peas cut on a angle, 1 red pepper seeded and julienne, 1 bunch chopped scallions, 2 cups lightly steamed bean sprouts, 1/4 cup ginger carrots, 1 can drained baby corn, heat for 2 minutes and serve while hot.

Ginger Carrots

Heat 1 tsp. oil in a wide frying pan stir in 4 cups diagonally sliced carrots, 1 cup water, 1/8 tsp. garlic powder, 1 tb. brown sugar ginger, 2 tb. white vinegar and 1/4 tsp. salt. Cover and simmer over medium high heat 12 to 10 minutes or until tender sprinkle with parsley.

My Photo/08

Stir Fried Beef and Broccoli

Mix 1/2 lb. steak cut in thin strips with 5 to 6 tb. oil, 1 tb. cornstarch, 2 tb. soy sauce. Stir in 1/4 tsp. sugar, let stand at room temperature for 30 minutes. With the remaining mixture add 2 tsp. sugar with 1 tb. dry sherry or lemon juice and 2 tsp. sesame oil, 1 tb. cornstarch and 1/3 cup cold water, mix and set aside. Heat a skillet over high heat, add 2 tb. oil and heat 30 seconds. Add 2 medium thinly sliced onions and fry for 2 minutes. Remove and set aside. Wipe pan add 1 tb. oil, heat and add meat and fry for 1 minute, add vegetables and stir to blend, add soy mixture to thicken.

My Photos/ 08

Asparagus Crab Swiss

Dressing............ Whisk together with 1 tb. Dijon mustard, 1 tb. lemon juice, 1 tb. vinegar, 1 egg yolk, 3 tb. olive oil and 2 tb. grated Parmesan cheese, whisk to mix add salt and pepper. Salad.............. 12 asparagus stems trimmed, cook in salted water for 2 to 3 minutes, rinse with cold water, pat dry. 2 heads endives leaves separated, arrange on plate. Top with asparagus, 2 Avocados, peeled, pitted and sliced, 1 julienned carrot, 12 oz. crab meat, 1 cup julienned Canadian Swiss Cheese, finely grated zest of lemon. Salt and pepper. Drizzle with dressing.

Nic's Photo/08

Salmon Loaf

Beat 2 eggs until frothy. Add 3 tb. lemon juice and beat again. Add instant onion flakes, 1 tb. butter 1 tsp. salt, and 1/4 tsp pepper. Clean the skin and bones from 2 7oz salmon, mix with egg and juice mixture. Add 3/4 cup milk and 2 cups bread crumbs, mix well. Pack into a greased loaf pan or a casserole dish. Bake in a 350 oven for 1 hour.

My Photo/ 08

Creamy Fish Fillets

In a sauce pan combine 2 tb. chicken bouillon with 1 qt. water, add 1 diced carrot, 1 cup diced potatoes, 1 cup diced celery, 1/2 cup chopped onion, 1/4 tsp. oregano, 1/4 tsp salt and pepper. Bring to a boil, drop the heat to a simmer for 10 to 15 minutes until vegetables are tender but firm, add 1 lb. fillets and cook 10 more minutes. In a sauce pan melt 1/4 cup butter, over medium heat, add 1/4 cup flour, slowly to blend, 1/2 tsp. salt, gradually add 2 cup milk, stir until thickened. Slowly add to the vegetable mixture stirring constantly until thickened. Serve while hot.

Nicky's Photo/.08

Fresh Almond Baked Trout

Cook 1/2 cup butter and 2/3 cup sliced almonds in a sauce pan until lightly browned, stir twice. Season a washed and dried Trout with 2 tsp. lemon juice, 1/4 salt and pepper. Arrange in a greased baking dish. Pour almond butter mixture over trout and cover. Bake in a 350 oven for 15 to 20 minutes or until fish flakes. Let stand for 5 minutes before serving.

Nic's Photo/08

Fish Casserole

Cook 1 tsp. grated onion in 4 tb. butter in top of double boiler blend in 4 tb. flour, 1 tsp. salt and a dash of pepper. Add 4 cups milk, 1/2 cup light cream, a dash of tabasco. Cook over boiling water, stirring constantly until thickened. In a bowl beat 4 eggs, add 1 tb. sherry wine or chicken broth, stir to blend evenly. Place 3 cups of fish of choice into a greased casserole dish, pour sauce over evenly. Bake in a 325 oven for 30 minutes, then sprinkle 1 cup buttered bread crumbs, bake for another 30 minutes or until a inserted knife comes out clean

47

Cindy's Photo

Potato Bannock

In a large bowl combine 2 1/2 cups sifted flour, 2 tb. baking powder, 2 tb. sugar, 1 tsp. salt. Cut in 1/4 cup shortening until mixture resembles course crumbs. With a fork stir in 1 cup milk and 1 cup cooled mashed potatoes. Move to a lightly floured board and knead gently for 8 to 10 times, working a little more flour if too sticky. Place dough on a greased baking sheet and pat with floured hands to form a large oval about 1 inch thick. Brush with milk. Bake in a 450 oven for 15 to 20 minutes or until golden brown, slice in to quarters and serve with butter.

Nics Photo/09

Sally Lunn Bread

Dissolve 1 pkg. active dry yeast in 1/4 cup warm water, add 1/4 cup warm milk and set aside. Cream, 3 tb. margarine with 1 1/2 tb. sugar. Add 2 eggs and alternately with yeast mixture. Sift 3 1/2 cups flour and 1 1/4 tsp. salt add to margarine mixture. Knead lightly, let rise in a warm place until double size. Punch down and knead lightly again, place in a well greased Sally Lunn mold or a angel food pan. Let rise again for 1 hour and bake for 1 hour in a 300 oven.

My Photos/08

111

Winter Tomato Sauce

Mince 1 onion, 1/3 cup celery and 1/4 cup carrot. Cook in a heavy skillet with 2 tb. olive oil on low heat, stirring until softened. Add 3 cloves of minced garlic and cook just until blended, about 1 minute. Add 1 can of coarsely pureed stewed tomatoes. Mix in 1/2 tsp. sugar, 1/4 tsp. thyme and 1 bay leaf, salt and pepper to taste. Bring to a boil, drop to a simmer for 10 to 15 minutes, stirring occasionally until slightly thickened. Discard the bay leaf and puree just until smooth add salt, pepper and sugar if needed. Store in fridge for 3 days or freeze for up to 2 to 3 months. use over any type of noodles or cook with any types of meats.

Nicky's Photo/08

Hot Brie Cheese Vins

Cut the top rind off the Brie with a sharp knife, place the Brie on a small oven baking dish. Cut cross wise on the thickest part of a pear, center on top of the Brie, surrounding the Brie with sliced blanched almonds. Broil the Brie under a heated broiler, 8 inches from the heat for 3 to 4 minutes, or until the Brie has softened, transfer carefully to a platter. Place slices of the remaining pair around the Brie. Place portions on top of sliced baguettes. Serve as a first course.

Sausage one Dish Meal

Prick and boil 1 lb. sauage for 10 minutes to remove fat. Wash, peel and slice 2 to 3 potatoes, layer slices over bottom of a greased casserole dish.. Add 1 sliced onion evenly, 2 to 3 peeled and sliced carrots evenly, potatoes then onions and carrots with 1 cup peas spread over evenly on top. Arrange sauage on top peas. In a bowl mix 1 can water with 1 can condensed tomato soup, pour over potato vegetable layers evenly and bake covered in a 350 oven for 1 hour. Remove cover and broil until sauage has browned about 8 to 10 minutes, watch closely as to not burn.

114

Chicken and Bacon Pie

Cut 1 lb. chicken into cubes, dice 4 strips of bacon. Heat 1 oz. butter and fry the bacon with 2 to 4 sliced mushroom for a few minutes. Heat 1 oz. butter in a sauce pan, sprinkle in 2 tb. flour and stir cooking until a smooth paste, stir in 1/2 cup milk and 1/2 cup chicken stock slowly, season and cook until thickened add the chicken, bacon and mushrooms. Place in a pie plate, cover with pie pastry, brush with beaten egg, bake in a 400 oven for 45 minutes.

My Photo/08

L'Orange Chicken

Lightly sprinkle lemon pepper over 4 boneless chicken breasts. Grill 8 to 10 minutes on each side, or until cooked. In a sauce pan, combine 1/3 cup brown sugar, 1/3 cup white sugar, 1/4 tsp. salt and 1 tb. corn starch, stir slowly, stir in 1 cup orange juice, 1 tsp. Dijon mustard. Simmer over medium heat and bring to a boil until transparent and thickened. Stir in drained mandarin oranges, heat slightly with out a boil. Spoon over cooked chicken.

116

My Photo/08

Lemon Chicken

Combine 1/4 cup lemon juice, 1/4 cup vegetable oil, 1/2 tsp. salt, 1/4 tsp. thyme and 1/8 tsp. pepper to make marinade. Pour over 1   2 1/2 lb. chicken cut in quarters. Marinate for 1 hour in refrigerator, drain chicken. Dust with 1/2 cup flour. Heat 1/4 cup oil in a heavy skillet. Fry chicken in hot oil and fry until golden in color on all sides. Bake in a 350 oven for 30 to 40 minutes until tender and cooked through.

Barbecued Chicken

Combine 1/2 tsp. poultry seasoning, 2 tb. lemon juice, 1/3 cup soy sauce, 1/4 cup catsup and 2 tb. vegetable oil for a marinade. Marinade for 1 to 2 hours. Barbecue 1 chicken sectioned into pieces, on medium heat until cooked through. Heat left over sauce until a simmer for 1 to 2 minutes and use for dipping.

Chicken Cacciatore

Brown 1   2 1/2 lb. cut up chicken in oil over medium heat. Remove chicken, add 1/2 cup chopped green onion, 1/2 cup chopped celery, 2 cloves chopped garlic, fry over medium heat, add 1 4 oz. can of button mushrooms, 1 1/2 cups canned tomato paste, 1/2 cup chicken broth, 2 tsp. sugar, salt and pepper. Add 2 1/2 cups water and chicken, cook over low heat until chicken has cooked through. Serve over noodles.

Sesame Chicken Nuggets

Cut up 16 oz. of skinless, boneless chicken breast into large cubes, wash and pat dry with paper towel, dip in sesame seeds to coat. Heat 2 tb. oil and brown on all sides. Cut up 4 cups red peppers sliced and washed. Add 4 oz. string snow peas and 4 oz. bean sprouts, washed and drained. Coarsely grate 1 tb. fresh ginger, add to chicken with 6 tb. chicken stock and 4 tsp. soy sauce, add red pepper, cover and cook for 3 minutes. Add snow peas and cook for 1 minute longer then add bean sprouts and stir just enough to heat through.

118

Cranberry Turkey Squares

Melt 2 tb. butter in a baking dish. Blend 1/2 cup sugar, 1 tsp. grated orange peel, cover with 2 cups cranberries. Combine 5 cups of cubed turkey, 1 cup turkey stock, 1 cup milk, 1 tsp. salt, 1/4 tsp. pepper, 2 tb. chopped onion, 2 cups left over turkey stuffing, or soft cubed bread and 2 slightly beaten eggs, mix thoroughly and pack firmly over cranberries. Bake at 400 for 45 minutes. Turn up side down on a serving dish, cut into squares and serve hot.

Tinas's Turkey Stew

Boil turkey carcass in a large pot for 1 to 2 hours. remove from water and cool enough to be able to remove the remaining meats, set aside. Strain any loose bone from broth and season with 2 tb. chicken broth, add turkey, 1 tsp. garlic, add salt and pepper to taste. Peel and cubed 3 medium potatoes, 2 carrots, 1 small 1/2 a rutabaga, 1 cup flowerets of broccoli and cauliflower with 1/2 chopped onion. Simmer on medium heat until cooked but still firm about 25 minutes. Thicken with flour and water mixture. Serve with baking powder biscuits.

My Photo/07

Turkey and Ham Casserole

In a heavy skillet, saute 1/2 cup chopped onion in 2 tb. butter until golden and tender, blend in 3 tb. flour, 1/2 tsp. salt, 1/4 tsp. pepper. Add 1 3 oz can sliced mushrooms, 1 cup light cream and 2 tb. dry sherry or chicken broth, cook over low heat, stir until thickened. Add 2 cups cooked, cubed turkey, 1 cup cooked, cubed ham and 1 5 oz. can drained and sliced water chestnuts, Pour into greased casserole dish. Sprinkle with 1/2 cup shredded Swiss cheese. Mix together 1 1/2 cups bread crumbs with 3 tb. melted butter and spread around the edge of casserole. Bake at 400 for 20 to 25 minutes or until lightly browned.

Pineapple Ham and Rice

Bring 1 1/2 cup pineapple juice to a boil. Stir in 1 1/2 cups instant rice, remove from heat let stand for 10 minutes. Fluff with a fork, set aside. In a heavy frying pan melt 1 tb. butter add 1/2 cup chopped onions, cook until soft, Cut 1 large ham steak into cubes add the pineapple chunks to cooked onions and slightly brown. Pour in rice with 1/2 cup frozen peas. Cover and drop heat to low and cook until peas has just warmed.

My Photo/07

Italian Sausage Casserole

Cut 2 lb. Italian Sausage into bite size pieces. Heat 2 tb. oil in a heavy pan. Add sausage and brown, remove with slotted spoon. Add 1 sliced onion and 2 crushed cloves of garlic to pan, saute over low heat until soft and browned, drain off excess oil. Return sausage with 1 19 oz. can tomatoes with juice, 1 7 oz. can tomato sauce and season with 2 tsp. basil, 1/2 tsp. oregano. Break up tomatoes. Cut 4 unpeeled potatoes into bite size pieces and stir in. Bring to a boil, cover and reduce heat, simmer for 20 to 25 minutes or until potatoes are tender, stirring as you go. Add 1 chopped green pepper. Turn into a baking dish. Sprinkle 1 1/2 cup grated c mozzarella cheese over top. Bake in a 350 oven for 20 to 30 minutes.

Baked Rice

Melt 2 tb. butter and saute 1/2 cup green pepper add 1 1/2 cup uncooked rice, 1 can button mushrooms with juice, 6 chopped green onions season with 1 tsp. oregano, 1/2 tsp garlic powder, 3 cans consomme and 2 cans water add 1 cup water later if needed. Bake in a 350 oven for 2 1/2 hours, fluff up with a fork and serve hot.

Sauage with Tomato Dumplinas

Slice your favorite sauage 1/4 inch thick slices. Saute in a deep pan with 1/4 cup chopped onion, 1/4 cup chopped celery until slightly browned. Add 1 can of tomatoes with 1 tsp. sugar, 1/2 tsp. salt, bring to a boil. In a medium size bowl combine 1 cup flour, 2 tsp. baking powder, 1 tsp. sugar, 1/2 tsp. salt, cut in 2 tb. cold margarine until crumbly add 1/2 cup milk, stir to mix. Drop by the spoon fulls over boiling sauage, drop heat to a simmer and cover and simmer for 15 to 20 minutes.

My Photo/08

123

Veal Goulash

Season 1 lb. veal cut in 1 inch cubes with salt and ginger, dip into flour to coat each piece on all sides. Brown in 2 tb. oil until browned evenly. Add 1 1/2 cups beef stock and 1 clove of garlic. Cover and cook in a 325 oven until tender, about 1 hour. Add a mixture of garden vegetables, cook for another 30 to 40 minutes or until vegetables are cooked through but firm. Thicken with a mixture of 1 tb. flour and 2 tb. of water. Pour a serving spoon full over flat bread, and eat while hot.

My Photo/07

Hungarian Veal

In a paper bag add 1/4 cup sifted flour, 2 tsp. salt, 1/8 tsp. pepper. Drop in 1 1/2 lb. of lean veal or venison cut in cubes until well coated. In a skillet with 2 tb. vegetable oil cook until browned. Stir in 1 1/2 cup water gradually. Add 10 to 12 pealed pearl onions, 1 small paired and diced eggplant. Cover and simmer until tender. Stir in 1 cup sour cream, 1 tsp. paprika. Turn in to a casserole dish Sprinkle with 1 cups of frozen hash browns evenly on top, dot with butter. Bake at 350 for 25 minutes. Serve with biscuits.

Garry's Photo/07

Hamburger Casserole

Melt 2 tb. butter in pan. Saute 1 lb. ground beef and 2 slices onion until browned. Add 1 cup tomato soup and 1/2 cup corn. Add 1 cup of cheesy macaroni. Mix thoroughly. Place in a greased baking dish. Cover with 1 cup mashed potato. Brush tops with egg yolk. Bake in a 450 oven until browned.

My Photo/07

Meat Balls and Dumplings

Season 1 1/2 lb. lean ground beef with 1 tsp. salt, 1/4 tsp. pepper and form into ping pong ball size. Heat 2 tb. oil in a heavy pan, add 1 sliced onion and meat balls, use a spoon to turn to brown on all sides. Cover with water and simmer for 30 to 40 minutes, remove meat add dumplings. Cover tightly and cook for 20 to 25 minutes. Remove dumplings to a hot platter with the meat. Mix flour and water to a smooth paste, add to water to make a gravy, simmer a mixture of vegetables until tender add meat and dumplings. Serve with biscuits.

Dumplings

Dumplings in a bowl mix 2 cups flour, 1 tsp. salt, 4 tsp. baking powder, 3 tb. margarine, mix until crumbly with hands. Add 3/4 cup milk gradually to make a soft dough. Drop from a spoon into hot gravy, cover with lid and simmer on a low heat on a simmer for 20 to 25 minutes with out lifting the lid. Cooked when firm to touch..

My Photos/08

Tina's Foxy Meatballs

Mix together 1 lb. lean ground beef with 1/4 cup minced onion, 1 minced garlic clove, 1 tsp. red relish, 1 tsp. mustard, 1 tsp. katshup, 1 tb. Parmesan cheese, 1 tb. fine bread crumbs, 1 tsp. salt and pepper. Incorporate well. form into balls. Cook meatballs in a heavy skillet until browned on all sides remove and keep warm. In skillet add 1 1/2 cup of beef broth, add 1 tb. of oyster sauce and simmer to loosen all browning from meatballs, strain. Return to a clean skillet. Mix 2 tb. flour to 3 tb. water in a jar, shake to mix well until smooth. Pour into beef broth and stir until thickened to a smooth gravy, add meatballs and simmer on low heat until meatballs are cooked. Serve with mashed potatoes

Garry's Photo/08

Sloppy Joe's

Ground Beef Mix

Brown 4 lb. ground beef, 2 large chopped onion, drain excess fat. Add 2 tsp. salt, 1/2 tsp. pepper and 1/2 tsp. garlic, cook slowly for 5 minutes, divide beef mixture into 2 cups and set aside.

In browning pan simmer 2 cups ground beef with 2 tb. brown sugar, 2 tb. vinegar, 1/2 cup catsup and 1 tb. prepared mustard for 10 minutes. Serve over buns. The remaining thoroughly cooled beef mix place in buggies or containers, label and date and freeze up to 3 months to use for another time.

My Photo/ 07

Stuffed Meat Loaf

Combine 1 egg, 1/3 cup milk, 1 cup bread crumbs, 1/4 cup finely chopped onion, 1 tsp. salt and pepper set aside for 4 to 5 minutes. Mix in 1 lb. lean ground beef until well incorporated. Place on wax paper and press into a 9 x 13 rectangle pan.

Stuffing mix 4 cups soft bread crumbs, 1/4 cup finely chopped onions, 1/2 tsp. sage, 1/2 tsp. Thyme and 2 to 4 tbsp. milk to moisten, mix thoroughly.

Spread stuffing over entire meat pat gently. Roll up starting with long side and seal edges. Place in a ungreased pan.

Bake at 350 for 45 to 50 minutes.

Garry's Photo/08

Nic's

130

Beef and Corn Bake

In a heavy pan brown 2 lb. ground beef break into small pieces add 1 medium chopped onion as its cooking and drain any grease. Turn into a large bowl with 1 can kernel corn, 2 cans condensed tomato soup, 1 tsp salt, 1/2 tsp. pepper, and 1 tb. ketchup, mix thoroughly. Mix in 2 cups cooked noodles, turn into a greased casserole dish, Top with 1 cup grated cheese cover and bake in a 350 oven for 45 minutes, remove lid and bake for another 10 minutes or until bubbly.

My Photo/08

Meat Loaf

Saute 1 medium chopped onion in 3 tb. oil. In a bowl mix 1/2 lb. lean ground beef with 1 egg, 1/3 cup uncooked oatmeal, 1/3 cup beef broth and season with 1 tsp salt, 1/2 tsp. pepper and 1/4 tsp. marjoram add onion, mix lightly. Shape mixture into a loaf and bake uncovered in a skillet at 350 for about 45 minutes to 1 hour. Cut with a serrated knife in thick slices and serve hot.

132

My Photo/05

Elegant Steak with Rice

Cut 1 1/2 lb. tenderized and boneless, round steak into thin strips. In a large heavy frying pan brown in 1 1/2 tb. oil on high. Add 2 onions sliced and separated into rings, saute until crisp and tender. Blend in 1 10 oz. can of cream mushroom soup, 1 can 10 oz. can sliced mushrooms with liquid. Add 1/2 cup beef broth, 1 crushed clove of garlic. Cover and simmer for 1 hour or until steak is tender. Serve over hot fluffy rice.

Cindys dragon fly/ My Graphics

Quick Beef Stroganoff

In a skillet cook 1/2 cup chopped onions in 4 tb. cooking oil until tender, move to the side. Cut 6 minute steaks into 1/2 inch wide strips and brown quckly, add more oil if needed. Mix 1 10 oz. can of cream of mushroom soup with 1 cup water, add to steak with 1 cup sour cream. Heat and season with 1 tsp. Worcestershire Sauce and garlic salt to taste. Serve over cooked egg noodles at once.

Nicky's Photo/07

134

pepper Steak

Precook 1 round steak cut in small steaks, in a beef broth in the oven at 350, Strain steak and set aside. Prepare onions, carrots, tomatoes cut in large chunks and 1 green pepper cut in strips cook in strained broth for 5 minutes add mushrooms and tomatoes. Later mix together 1/4 cup water, 1/4 cup soy sauce and 2 tb. cornstarch add to vegetable mixture. cook until thickened. Add cooked meat,add chopped tomatoes and mushrooms, place in a 350 oven for 30 to 35 minutes longer.

My Photo/07

Beef Rollups

Trim off any fat on 4 slices of round steak and flatten with a meat mallet. In a bowl combine 1/2 cup cottage cheese, 2 tb. grated Romano cheese, 1 minced onion, 3 tb. chopped parsley, 2 tsp. oregano, 1/2 tsp. salt, 1/2 clove of garlic and 1 egg. Spread the filling over the steak. Roll beef jellyroll style. Place rollups with seam side down in a shallow baking dish just large enough to hold them in place. Combine 1 cup tomato sauce with 1/4 cup red wine and pour over beef. Bake in a 350 oven for 1 hour and baste occasionally.

My Photo/08

English Meat Pie

In a heavy frying pan saute 1 cup chopped onions in oil until onions are transparent add 1 lb. lean round steak, lean pork cut in 3/4" cubes, sear with out browning, sprinkle 1 tb. flour over meat and stir in. Add 1/2 lb. small cleaned and halved mushrooms, salt and pepper to taste, 1 10 oz. can consomme and 1 1/4 cup boiling water simmer for 15 to 30 minutes. Roll out dough on a floured board to 1/4 inch thick, fit in a casserole dish. Pour filling into casserole dish. Roll remaining dough to fit top making a gash in the centre. Seal dough with finger tips. Brush top with a mixture of 1 egg yolk with 1 tsp water.   Bake at 425 for 15 minutes, reduce heat to 350 for 1/2 hour reduce heat again to 250 and bake for 1 1/2 hours. serves 6 to 8.

137

Cindy's Photo/ 07

Beef Bourguignon

In a skillet add 2 tb. olive oil. Saute 2 lb. round steak cut into 1 inch cubes until browned on all sides. Transfer beef to a large oven proof casserole dish. In the skillet saute 2 cups chopped onions, 4 medium peeled and chunk size carrots, 2 chopped celery sticks and 2 minced garlic cloves until onions are translucent, add to the casserole with the beef. In the same skillet, combine 2 cups burgundy wine, 1 14 oz. can beef broth, 1 tb. catsup, 2 tb. Worcestershire sauce, 1/2 tsp salt, 1/4 tsp pepper, 1/2 tsp. thyme. In a cup mix 1/4 cup flour with 1/2 cup water mix until smooth add to wine mixture, stirring constantly until it comes to a boil, pour over meat mixture, add 1 can drained sliced mushrooms. Cover and bake in a 350 oven for 3 hours or until meat is tender. Prepare 1 box of wide egg noodles to the package directions. Serve the beef bourguignon over the noodles.

My Photos/07

Country Beef stew

Cut 2 lb. chuck steak, cut into 1 inch cubes, braise on all sides in hot oil, stir often. Add 2 cup hot water, 1 tsp. Worcestershire sauce, 1 mashed clove of garlic, 1 small sliced onion, Season with salt and pepper to taste and simmer on a medium low heat for 1 1/2 hours, stirring occasionally to stop any sticking . Add four peeled and sliced carrots, 4 diced potatoes and 1 cup of chopped turnip, and 1 cup of chopped celery, cover and simmer for 30 minutes. Thicken with flour or cornstarch mixture.

My Photos/ Nick's Graphics

Saucy Venison Medallions

Make a tangy sauce mixture of 2 grated lemons, with juice. 1 tsp. crushed peppercorns and 1 tsp. thyme. Pound lightly, 12 venison pieces from the loin 3 inches long and 1 1/2 in. thick with a mallet hammer and marinate in the mixture for several hours at room temperature, pat dry. In a heavy skillet brown the disks in 2 tb. butter, a few at a time adding olive oil if needed, don't over cook.

Transfer to a heated plater and keep warm. Pour off any oils from browning. Add 1/4 cup balsamic vinegar, 1 cup red wine, bring to a boil, stirring to dissolve the browning on pan. Add 1 cube beef stock, thicken with 2 tb. corn starch mixed with 2 tb. cold water, stir into wine mixture until thickened. Pour over cooked medallions, serve hot.

Nic's barn/08

140

Glazed Pheasant with Wild Rice

Wash and dry a disjoined Pheasant. Dip in 1 beaten egg and roll in 1/4 cup flour. Heat 1/4 cup oil in a heavy skillet, fry the pieces of pheasant until lightly browned on all sides. In a sauce pan mix 2 cups syrup from canned pineapple, 1 tb. butter, 2 tb. cooking sherry, dash salt and 1 tb. cornstarch. Cook until thickened, pour over browned pheasant. Reduce heat, cover and simmer for 1 hour or until tender. Serve with wild rice with a mixed vegetable.

Nic's Photo/ My Graphics

Buffalo Jump Chili

In a heavy skillet brown and break up 3 lb. ground bison into small pieces until quite fine, add 2 medium size chopped onions, cook until onions are transparent. Add 3 chopped Poblano peppers, mix in to incorporate. Add 3 30 oz.. can diced tomatoes, 3 to 4 tb. chilli powder, 1 1/2 tsp. cumin, 1 1/2 tsp. paprika, 3 cloves crushed garlic and the juice from 1 squeezed lime. Add water just to cover. Simmer on low heat for 1 to 1 1/2 hours.

142

My Photo 08

Western Baked Beans

Add 3 chopped onions, 1/2 cup brown sugar, 1 tsp. dry mustard, 1/2 tsp. garlic powder, 1 tsp. salt, 1/2 cup cider vinegar in a skillet, cover and cook on a medium low heat for 20 minutes. Add simmered onions and liquids to a 2 qt. casserole dish with 1 19 oz.. can lima beans, 1 28 oz.. can kidney beans, 1 19 oz.. can chick peas and 1 28 oz.. can baked beans, cover and bake in a 350 oven for 30 minutes, uncover and bake for another 30 minutes more.

Nicky's Photo/08

143

IN & AROUND
BC
&
ALBERTA

144

Nic's Graphics

Index

145

My husband Garry. He is my pilot, he has taught me the love of nature and takes me to places where we explore its beauty together.

My daughter Cindy. For her encouragement to continually learn and try new techniques. She motivates me.

My daughter Nicole. For her fine touches to my graphic arts and for her unwavering support during our late nights together creating these books.

Note for Librarians: A cataloguing record for this book is available from Library
and Archives Canada at www.collectionscanada.ca/amicus/index-e.html

Printed in Victoria, BC, Canada.

ISBN: 978-1-4251-8510-7 (sc)

Library of Congress Control Number:

*Our mission is to efficiently provide the world's finest, most comprehensive book publishing
service, enabling every author to experience success. To find out how to publish your book, your
way, and have it available worldwide, visit us online at www.trafford.com*

Trafford rev. 8/28/2009

www.trafford.com

North America & international
toll-free: 1 888 232 4444 (USA & Canada)
phone: 250 383 6864 ♦ fax: 812 355 4082